LOGGED IN, CHECKED OUT

BOOST PRODUCTIVITY AND IMPROVE COMMUNICATION

NICOLE HOLLAR

Mindset Press, LLC

This content was originally featured in the bestselling leadership anthology When Work Works (2024), where Nicole Hollar was selected as a contributing author. It has been reimagined and expanded here as a standalone guide for leaders who are ready to improve communication, protect time and energy, and lead productive, focused teams.

ISBN: 979-8-9883168-3-1 (Paperback)
ISBN: 979-8-9883168-4-8 (eBook)

Published in Fort Lauderdale, FL

Cover designer and interior layout: Charlyn Samson
Cover image: DjelicS

Visit the author's website for purchases, bookings, and workshops:

www.nicolehollar.com

CONTENTS

Workplaces function best when
everyone on the team is mindful,
has healthy boundaries, and
demonstrates respect.

While speaking at a recruitment event for teenage athletes—their sport was basketball—I explained to them that the lessons they learn on the court would influence their lives. During that time, I commended them for being at the event and having a commitment to improving their skills as individuals and team players. Much like those teen athletes, you are also a player on a team at work. Who is relying on you to show up today? Who are you relying on?

During my talk, I told the audience that not every person in the room will be the high scorer, or the best ball handler, or have the expert vision to set up a play. Yet, they all had an important role, and each one, much like you, could not succeed without the rest of the team.

It's not just about showing up, however. It is about committing to being present, communicating your needs and being open to hearing those of others when you are on the court in the workplace.

As an empowerment and growth coach, I show people how capable they are and give them the necessary tools to evolve and grow. Recently, my *Breakthrough Coaching* client, Jessica, and I discussed a situation at work that often leaves her and her coworkers frustrated. She is not meeting timeline expectations, and her coworkers are not cooperating with her in a way that would help her meet the demands of her job. Jessica's role in marketing has her wearing many hats, keeping her busy moving about the office and attending virtual meetings in addition to creating actual marketing products.

The root of their collective problem was a combination of ineffective communication, lack of personal awareness and accountability, stubbornness, wasted time, and an absence of planning.

Jessica, who worked in an office for at least half of the week, often found herself in hallway conversations where people told her what they needed, or asked how a project was going, which she often could not give a status update about because it wasn't even in her queue. For Jessica, on-the-fly hallway conversations where coworkers advised her of their marketing needs were ineffective. For this reason, she would ask people to send her an email about what they needed so she could see it while at her computer, versus a passing conversation while walking down the hall, her mind cluttered and on her way elsewhere—often to meetings which she described as "a frequent waste of my time."

For teams to function best,
individuals must have quality
communication, know their roles,
and be accountable for their actions.

They must also be mindful about what they really need from the people around them, and that their top priority may not be another person's.

COMMUNICATE LIKE A BENDY STRAW —

To communicate your needs, it is great if you know how someone prefers to receive information so you can deliver it most effectively. Knowing how you learn is also important, so you can explain how you best receive information. Jessica, for example, knew she needed tasks written down and routinely asked for work requests in email form.

If you have an ongoing fight involving not remembering an important date, and you know you need it written down and not delivered in conversation on the fly, tell the person. Likewise, if someone wants to remember and has asked you to write it down, even if it is not what you need to recall an item, do it. Those are examples of behavioral flexibility.

KNOW YOUR LEARNING STYLE ⸺

There are four primary modes of learning: watching, listening, doing, and assimilating data. In school, many science or work-study programs utilize multiple learning methods. First, students learn in the classroom, usually by listening to the instructor and reading the material, followed by a hands-on practicum where they get to apply their skills.

Primary Modes of Learning

Visual (V): Seeing it or reading it.

Auditory (A): Listening to its explanation.

Kinesthetic (K): Doing it or being hands-on.

Auditory Digital (Ad): Getting all the data in various ways to assimilate.

When you listen to people speak, listen to the phrases they use. This will often give you an idea of their preferred learning method. "I love when people *tell me* about the specs on a car," or "*I read* about all the car specs online."

Imagine college students—some retain information best by *reading* the textbook, while others prefer only to attend the lecture and *listen* to capture the information. Yet another student may need to *re-write* all the information to capture it, and someone else may need to *teach it*. In order, these examples illustrate learners who are *visual, auditory, auditory digital,* and *kinesthetic*. Most people have two top learning preferences depending on the topic.

> **To help you get a handle on your preferred learning style, order the following below, with 1 being MOST like you and 4 being LEAST like you. Note your two highest-ranking numbers as primary learning preferences.**
>
> _____ Reading books, studies, academia, maps, etc. (**V**isual)
>
> _____ Listening to stories or explanations. (**A**uditory)
>
> _____ Being hands-on/Doing the exercise (**K**inesthetic)
>
> _____ Understanding the relevance of the topic. The why? (**A**uditory **D**igital)

Knowing this information will allow you to properly communicate your needs and remind you to ask others how they prefer to receive the information you need to convey.

ASK FOR CLARITY

While some deliverables require a specific method or process, many do not. There will be times when someone may ask you for a deliverable or request something in a way that is not necessary for you, or not how you would do it. You get to decide whether yielding the end goal of the project or team is most important, or standing firm in your own methods is most important.

In the case of Jessica, who I mentioned earlier, she specifically and frequently asked people to communicate with her in written form, yet coworkers continued to tell her their needs during informal verbal conversations. It might not be what they needed, but it is what she needed. You can choose to be flexible in your delivery methods or not.

Empathy is an
underused skill.

People are most successful and productive when communication is clear. Asking for clarity will help all parties involved be most successful and feel accomplished.

If you find that even after communicating your needs, you are not receiving information in your preferred learning style, what can you do to help yourself? In the case of Jessica, it was simple: she decided to carry an old-school notepad for people who were just not good at emailing. In her case, she knew that adding a task to her mobile device would likely result in her overlooking it. She was aware of who she was and her working style. So, she opted for a notepad because, to her, it symbolized work that needed to be done. Each day, she would transpose items to her master calendar. Jessica opted to contribute to the global goal instead of stubbornly insisting that if she didn't get an email, she wouldn't create the necessary marketing material.

I'M HERE, YOU'RE HERE ─────────

Whether you are in a hallway conversation, an important meeting, or feel trapped by a virtual "show and tell," focus on what is right in front of you. It is easy to become distracted by the environment you are in, or by the cascading thoughts and endless task lists running through your mind. But, because the brain takes in two million bits per second (bps), and our mind can only process 126 bps, you are wasting precious resources when you are distracted from the task at hand or the person in front of you.

To help you focus, imagine for a moment that you are in a movie dream sequence and everything outside of your immediate visual field falls away or into a blur. Give the speaker in front of you the courtesy you would want when delivering information, allowing other stuff to fade around you. Furthermore, don't distract other people who are trying to listen with sidebar chatter about its content, participants, the host, or another topic altogether.

You may find that by staying even fifty percent more present, the rest of what you want to accomplish in the day becomes easier because you are training your mind to stay focused and on task. Then, after the meeting, you can spend five to ten minutes with a coworker reviewing the positive takeaways or absurdities you just witnessed.

When I am speaking at organizations and the group is small enough, a tool I use to keep people engaged is asking intentional and planned questions. These questions can be used to confirm, clarify, or help shape the direction of the event. Periodic long pauses are another great way to engage people because they change the cadence of sound and break the rhythmic lull of continuous speaking.

MEETING THAT COULD HAVE BEEN AN EMAIL

How many meetings have you been in that really could have been emails? And how many emails have you received that did not need the "Reply All" button clicked? Before you schedule a meeting, there are some considerations that will make it more productive and its participants more focused and engaged.

Make meetings better and more productive with the following considerations:

1. Is it necessary?

   • Ask yourself, does everyone I am inviting really need to know the information I am sharing, or do I just want an audience?

   • Could I use feedback from everyone I am inviting?

   • Are there critical people I have left out?

   • Do Stacy and the other seventy people on this email chain need to know that I am attending Steve's meeting? Or can I save them from another "ding" and moment of unnecessary distraction by avoiding the "Reply All" button?

2. Have an agenda and set expectations for participants. Let them know why they are there.

    • I need you as a sounding board.

    • I am going to give you information to act on.

    • We are going to discuss a path towards...

    • Let's brainstorm ideas about...

    • I'd like to get your thoughts on/run by you...

    • We will decide...

3. Streamline the meeting to keep people focused.

    • Provide a brief outline.

    • Discuss high-priority items first.

    • Consider questions people may have and answer them as you go.

    • Hold off on taking additional questions from participants until the end.

4. Adapt the presentation to your audience without changing who you are.

    • Note whether you have a group that needs a slide deck to *see* or can just *listen.*

    • Is it best if they *take notes* for future reference? Tell them.

- Would it benefit your meeting's goal to provide a bullet point summary of key takeaways for them to *assimilate*?

5. Participate if you have been asked to join the meeting.

   - Stay off your phone or computer for the purpose of looking up other things or catching up from the previous meeting that did not have your full attention.

   - Your full presence will improve comprehension and meeting speed because you are not asking the presenter to repeat themselves. Instead, you can ask questions or participate in a way that can expedite or enhance the meeting.

6. Set expectations.

   - Tell participants the next action item post-meeting and expected due dates, if any.

   - Likewise, if the due dates are not realistic, tell the meeting host promptly so reasonable adjustments can be made.

YOUR BOUNDARY OR MINE? ——————

Learning to set boundaries requires an understanding of the entire situation and consideration for others. While boundary setting is you-centric, that doesn't mean that it's selfish. To have fluid relationships in any realm of life, empathy is necessary to create harmony. It's a moving dance involving stating your needs while respecting those of other people.

I DID THIS

Often, people create expectations for themselves that escalate, and they don't know how to get out of them. For example, answering work messages and emails at all hours is generally something self-created. The more it is done, the more people expect you to be on-demand. Or perhaps you have a growing amount of work meant for two people and the only way to complete it is by working longer and longer hours. If no one knows you are sinking—and even if they do, in some cases—there is little motivation to hire more people or redistribute the workload if possible. Then, one day, overworking finally burns you out or you become resentful. If being on-demand or having a seventy-hour workweek is an actual expectation of your company, ask yourself if you knew it from the outset and if it was within your boundaries then. If so, why is burning out okay?

BE MINDFUL

If you are someone who often sends stream-of-consciousness late-night emails, don't expect a reply until the next day. Your fire drill is not theirs. Yes, stuff happens at times. If you are someone who does this and didn't expect a reply, but you get one, remind the person that they are not obligated to violate their work-life boundary if they are doing so. Many people step over their personal line because of fear.

OPEN THE DANCE FLOOR

When discussing wellness with people, I often discover that many people do not snack during the day, something necessary to maintain glucose levels in the brain, alertness, and an elevated metabolism. Many people tell me that no one eats in a meeting, be it live or virtual, so they don't want to. I ask if it is an actual rule or just something you don't see. Then I remind them that someone needs to open the dance floor. When setting a boundary—like deciding you are going to eat your snacks, even during a meeting— you should still be courteous. Don't select smelly foods, like fish, or loud ones, like raw carrots; find something that will satisfy your needs and be mindful. Usually, once someone starts snacking during a meeting, others follow.

LEARN TO SHIFT

Whether boundary overreach is self-created or due to other circumstances, you have the right to set new ones at any time. For example, if you have allowed yourself to be the go-to person for everything in your department out of goodwill, allowing it to interfere with your actual job, you have the right to decline at any time. Honor that you have been a valuable resource for a long time, and remind people that they are resourceful enough to find an alternative solution, explaining that the extra work is interfering with your job performance. Just like values, boundaries may also change.

To help you become more productive at the beginning of each day, once you are at work (which might be at a designated workspace in your home), allocate twenty minutes to get a big-picture plan for your day or work on a pressing project. Once you've done that, check your emails and address other agenda items.

This new strategy may also mean sending people out of your office or going right to your desk without lingering. Most people report that it takes a couple of days for people to understand and accept that the first twenty minutes at work is your uninterrupted focus time. Here is your first chance to teach people your new boundary. Because people need to adapt to new boundaries, you must give them a little leeway to get used to your new ones.

REVIEW LIKE A FOOTBALL TEAM ───────

Be like a football team that reviews each game so they can make needed adjustments as they go. They don't wait until the end of the season. Most people are subject to an annual review of some sort, often determining raises, bonuses, and promotions.

Don't wait for a year or more to receive a formal review or feedback. Seek feedback periodically from peers, supervisors, and subordinates, or give it to those same groups. Occasional constructive feedback gives a person an opportunity to improve, show interest in growth, get a boost of positive praise, and provides other people with the floor to air any concerns before they escalate.

STEP AWAY FROM THE CANVAS ───────

Like an artist stepping back from his canvas to see the whole picture, every now and again, it is important to check in by stepping out. Look inward and ask yourself:

- Am I committing to being my best self?

- Can I improve how and when I communicate?

- Am I listening to what others are telling me?

- Am I focused?

- Does my contribution move the needle?

- Am I mindful that I am not the only person with needs and demands?

- Is there anything I can do to improve team unity or morale?

- What is bothering me, and is there a way I can address it appropriately?

The workplace is a social construct like any other, so it is important to recognize that you are a collection of people working independently and together to accomplish similar goals. By understanding and communicating your needs, creating and respecting boundaries, and engaging in quality feedback, the workplace becomes a better functioning, more respectful team environment.

APPENDIX: PRODUCTIVITY
TOOLS FOR TEAM LEADERS ───────

These tools are designed to help you apply the key principles from this book: better communication, stronger boundaries, and smarter leadership. Use them with your team or adapt them into your systems and workflows.

TOOL 1: PRODUCTIVE MEETING PREP &
FOLLOW-UP TEMPLATES ───────

Pre-Meeting Email Template

Subject: [Meeting Topic] – Goals, Prep, and Outcomes

Hi [Team/Name],

Ahead of our [meeting name] on [date/time], I wanted to share our objectives and a few quick notes to help us stay focused and efficient:

Purpose:

[One sentence – "To review Q2 project progress and resolve roadblocks."]

Key Outcomes:

- [Decision or discussion point #1]

- [Decision or discussion point #2]

- [Input or ideas needed on _____]

Prep Needed (if any):

- [Review the attached deck]

- [Bring your department's numbers]

Start and End Time:

We'll begin at [time] and wrap by [time].

Thanks for staying focused — this helps us respect everyone's time.

Best,
[Your Name]

Post-Meeting Follow-Up Template

Subject: Recap and Next Steps – [Meeting Name]

Hi [Team/Name],

Thanks for a productive discussion during our [meeting name] today. Below is a quick recap and agreed next steps:

Key Takeaways:

- [Major decision #1]

- [Major insight #2]

Next Steps & Owners:

- [Task 1] – [Name], due by [date]

- [Task 2] – [Name], due by [date]

Check-In Date:

We'll regroup on [date], or sooner if needed.

Thanks again,
[Your Name]

TOOL 2: MY COMMUNICATION SNAPSHOT (LEADER EXAMPLE) ————

Use this with your team to reduce miscommunication, encourage behavioral flexibility, and create shared expectations.

Name:

Role/Department:

Preferred Communication Style:

☐ Email ☐ Slack/Chat ☐ Verbal ☐ Written docs

When I'm Most Focused:

(e.g., mornings, after lunch)

How I Like to Receive Requests:

(e.g., calendar invite, subject line with deadline)

My Top Two Learning Preferences:

☐ Visual ☐ Auditory ☐ Kinesthetic ☐ Auditory Digital

One Thing That Helps Me Stay Productive:

(e.g., no-meeting mornings, short recaps)

My Commitment to the Team:

"I'll do my best to communicate clearly and respect how others receive information."

TOOL 3: BOUNDARY RESET SCRIPT ——

Use this when you need to reinforce after-hours boundaries without sounding dismissive or unhelpful.

Sample Auto-Response (email or chat):

Hi [Name], thanks for your message. I saw this come through after hours, and I'll review and respond during my regular work window [tomorrow morning/by X time]. Appreciate your patience!

Signature Line Options to Normalize Boundaries:

I may send emails outside of standard hours — please don't feel obligated to respond until your workday begins.

TOOL 4: TASK INTAKE FORM ——————

Use this format to reduce vague task requests and eliminate hallway drop-ins. You can send it as a reply or integrate it into project workflows.

Task Intake Questions:

- What do you need?

- By when?

- Why is this needed?

- What format do you prefer (slide, spreadsheet, summary)?

- Who else is involved or impacted?

TOOL 5: FIRST 20-MINUTE DAILY FOCUS SHEET

Use this as a self-leadership habit. It creates clarity before your inbox or calendar takes over.

Morning Focus:

- Today's #1 priority: _____

- One thing I will finish before noon: _____

- What could derail my focus today?: _____

- Boundary I will reinforce today: _____

- One person I'll support or check in with: _____

- How I'll know today was productive: _____

ABOUT THE AUTHOR ─────────────

Nicole Hollar is a dynamic speaker, coach, and advocate for personal growth and empowerment. Her best-selling book, *Feeling Stuck? Empower Yourself to Live a Happier, More Fulfilling Life,* is modeled after one of her highly successful one-to-one coaching programs, while her *OWN IT Podcast* furthers her quest to encourage people to take charge of their life, own their stuff, and get out of their way.

With more than two decades of experience in wellness and personal development, Nicole inspires individuals to unlock their full potential and live as their authentic selves.

Drawing from her background in wellness, neuro-linguistic programming, and Mental and Emotional Release®, Nicole brings an insightful approach to her coaching. Her ability to connect with clients fosters trust and enables them to make meaningful breakthroughs in their lives.

As a sought-after speaker, Nicole captivates audiences with her engaging style and relatable stories. Whether delivering keynotes, leading workshops, or facilitating group discussions, she shares practical strategies and transformative insights that resonate with diverse audiences.

Learn more about Nicole's coaching, book her for speaking engagements, and find empowering resources at her website:

www.nicolehollar.com

BOOKS

*Feeling Stuck? Empower Yourself to Live
a Happier, More Fulfilling Life*

When Work Works

*Grilled Cheese and Tasting Menus:
Stories of Growth and Change*

Connect with Nicole

Linktr.ee/
nicolehollar

Learn. Grow. Inspire.®

NOTES

NOTES

www.ingramcontent.com/pod-product-compliance
Lightning Source LLC
Chambersburg PA
CBHW071533210326
41597CB00018B/2985